Living in

ROMAN
TIMES

Jane Chisholm
Illustrated by Rob McCaig
History adviser: Dr Anne Millard
Designed by Kim Blundell

Contents

First published in 1982 by Usborne Publishing Ltd,
20 Garrick Street, London WC2E 9BJ, England.
Copyright © 1982 Usborne Publishing Ltd.
The name Usborne and the device ☺ are Trade Marks of Usborne Publishing Ltd.
Printed in Belgium by Henri Proost, Turnhout, Belgium.

Julius and his city

This book is all about a nine year old boy called Julius Valerius Cato. He lives in the city of Rome in Italy. The story takes place nearly 2,000 years ago. This was long before things like electricity, cars, aeroplanes or television were invented. The people who lived in Rome were called Romans. They spoke a language called Latin. The Romans had a huge army and ruled over most of Europe.

This is Julius and his pet dog, Brutus. Like most Romans, Julius lives in a flat. Only very rich people can afford houses of their own.

Julius's parents are called Antonius and Livia. Antonius works as a banker, lending people money.

Julius has a 15 year old brother, Caius*, and two sisters, Octavia, aged seven and Julia, aged 13.

Several slaves live in the flat too. They do the cooking and the housework and look after the children. A slave is someone who is owned by another person. There are a lot of slaves in Rome. They do all the hard jobs. Many are people from other countries, who were captured by the Romans during wars.

2   *Caius is pronounced Ky-us.

Capitol Hill. This is one of seven hills in Rome.

The baths

This is the temple where Julius's family go to pray. The Romans believe in many different gods and have lots of temples.

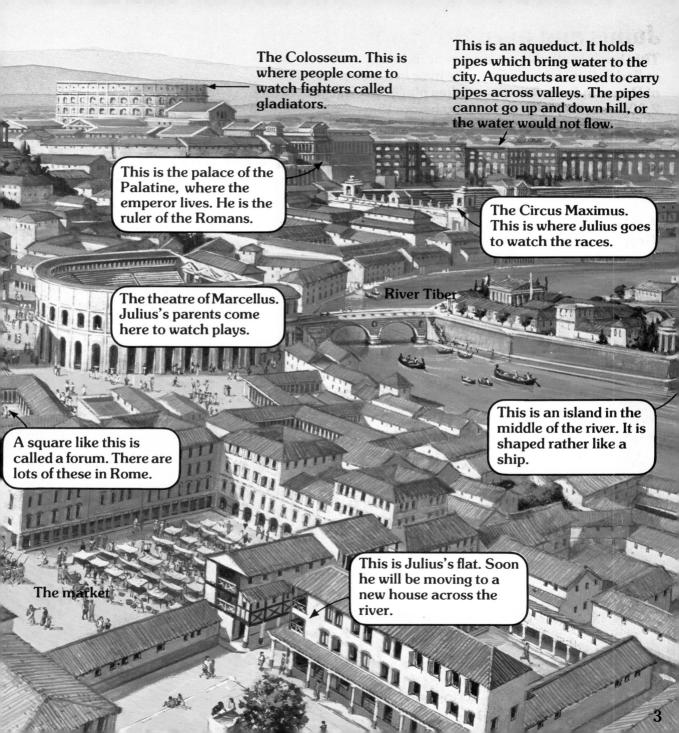

The Colosseum. This is where people come to watch fighters called gladiators.

This is an aqueduct. It holds pipes which bring water to the city. Aqueducts are used to carry pipes across valleys. The pipes cannot go up and down hill, or the water would not flow.

This is the palace of the Palatine, where the emperor lives. He is the ruler of the Romans.

The Circus Maximus. This is where Julius goes to watch the races.

River Tiber

The theatre of Marcellus. Julius's parents come here to watch plays.

This is an island in the middle of the river. It is shaped rather like a ship.

A square like this is called a forum. There are lots of these in Rome.

This is Julius's flat. Soon he will be moving to a new house across the river.

The market

3

The street where Julius lives

This is the block of flats where Julius lives. It is built around a courtyard. Julius's flat is on the first floor. It does not have a name or number. Only the main streets in Rome have names. So it is quite easy to get lost.

A night-watchman patrols the streets at night, making sure the buildings are locked. He has to keep a sharp look out for burglars too.

Opposite the flat is the barber's shop. Julius's father goes there to have his hair cut. It is a good place to meet friends and hear the latest news.

This is Julius's friend, Cornelius. His family rent the flat above from Julius's father.

Julius's bedroom

Baker's shop. Bread is baked here every morning.

Barber's shop

4

This is the dining room. The Romans have their meals lying on couches.

The artist has cut away the walls so you can see the rooms inside the flat.

Tavern

Most people get their water here. A few flats have their own water supply. The owners pay to have pipes connected to the fountain.

The tavern is a noisy, lively place. It sells drinks and cheap, hot meals. Many of the poorer people do not have kitchens in their flats. They eat here instead.

There are no toilets in Julius's flat. But there are some on the ground floor, which are shared by everyone in the block.

Getting up

Julius shares a bedroom with his brother Caius. One of the slaves wakes them when it is time to get up. It is still dark, so he lights an oil lamp.

Everyone gets up early in Rome. The streets start to bustle with people even before it is light. There are no clocks or watches, so no-one knows exactly what the time is. There are no street lights, but people carry lanterns to see by.

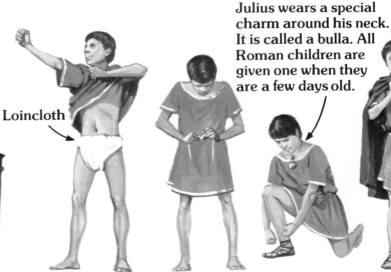

Loincloth

Julius wears a special charm around his neck. It is called a bulla. All Roman children are given one when they are a few days old.

Julius washes his face and hands. He rubs his teeth with his fingers and a special kind of powder.

Then he puts on a clean tunic and laces his leather sandals. When it is cold, he wears a short cloak too. It is very hot in Rome for most of the year, so people do not need to wear many clothes.

Octavia's tunic is made of cool, thin material. Poorer children wear tunics of cheaper material that feels rough and itchy.

She has a woollen belt around her waist.

Shawl

Leather sandals

Octavia puts on a long tunic with a thin tunic underneath. On top of this she wears a shawl. Roman girls dress just like their mothers.

The nurse combs her hair and plaits it for her. Octavia looks at herself in the mirror. It is made of polished silver. Mirror glass has not been invented.

Toga

Julius's father wears a toga over his tunic when he goes out. This is a large piece of cloth which he wraps round his body in a special way. Slaves and people from other countries are not allowed to wear togas.

Every morning the family prays together in the hall. They stand in front of the household shrine. This is the home of the gods who look after the family. The children bring food and drink to offer to the gods.

Going to school

Julius is taken to school by his personal slave, Titus. His friend, Cornelius goes with them. They do not have a proper breakfast. Instead they buy some bread to eat on the way. To get to school they walk along the river. There are barges of wheat being unloaded at the docks.

Roman girls do not go to school. Julia and Octavia are taught at home by their mother. They learn to read, write and run a house. A music teacher comes to give Julia lessons.

Theatre of Marcellus

Warehouses

These animals have been brought by ship from Africa. They will be used in fights to entertain the public.

Sacks of wheat from Egypt

Julius's classroom is above a shop. The school is run by a Greek teacher, called Perseus. There is only one class.

8

Statue of a famous writer.

Roman numbers look different from ours. These are the numbers from one to ten.

I II III IV V VI VII VIII IX X

Books are written on scrolls – long rolls of papyrus (a kind of paper).

Caius goes to a secondary school. Here he is learning how to speak in public. Romans think this is very important. He also learns Latin grammar, history, maths and Greek.

The children write on boards covered with wax. They use a pointed stick called a stylus. The flat end is used for rubbing out.

An abacus for doing sums. You slide the wooden balls along the wire as you count.

There are five boys in Julius's class. Most of them started going to school when they were six. They learn reading, writing and sums. Julius's father has to pay the teacher.

Many Roman children do not go to school as their parents cannot afford it. The teacher is strict. He beats the boys if they do not remember their lessons.

9

After school

School finishes at about midday. Then Julius and his friends are free to play games in the streets. There is no danger of being run over. Horse-drawn carts and chariots are the only things the Romans have to travel in. These are not allowed in Rome during the day.

The baths

The library. Julius's father sometimes comes here to read about the history of Rome.

Very rich people travel around in carrying chairs, called litters.

Julius and a friend are playing at being gladiators – special fighters who entertain the public.

The boys buy a snack lunch from a shop selling hot food. They have bread, cheese and sausages.

10

This is Senate House. Politicians called senators meet here to discuss government matters.

The law courts are in this building called the Basilica Aemilia. People like Julius's father also come here to do business.

This is the temple of Julius Caesar, a famous Roman leader.

The boys are not in a hurry to get home. They persuade Titus to take them into the city to explore. They go to the Roman Forum, the main forum in the centre of Rome. There are a lot of temples and other important buildings here. A politician is making a speech. He is a popular man and a lot of people have gathered to hear him.

On the way back, the boys visit Uncle Claudius, who is an army officer. He takes them to the barracks to watch the soldiers training. Like many Roman boys, Julius wants to go into the army one day.

Julius gets home at about four o'clock. He finds his sisters and their friends in the courtyard. They are playing knucklebones, a game rather like dice. You play with four pieces of bone with numbers on each side.

11

The public baths

There is a pool with very hot water in here.

Cold outdoor pool

Warm indoor pool

Like many Roman men, Julius's father spends most afternoons at the baths. (Women can go in the mornings.) Hardly anyone has a bath at home. People go there to meet friends, not just to wash or swim. There are several different pools, indoors and out. The water varies from very cold to steaming hot. The baths have shops, a library and a sports ground attached to them. Caius goes running and jumping in the sports ground. It is important for him to keep fit. He will be joining the army when he is sixteen.

Before having a swim, Antonius does some wrestling.

Then he goes into the hottest room, the steam room. The steam makes you sweat all the dirt out.

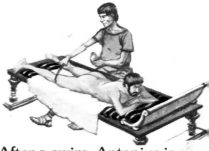

After a swim, Antonius is scrubbed clean by his slave. The slave rubs oil on his skin. Then he scrapes it off with a special scraper.

12

The evening

There is no chimney, so the kitchen gets quite smoky.

The cooking pots are made of clay. They break easily but are cheap to buy.

Julius and Octavia have their supper in the kitchen at about six o'clock. The cooks are busy preparing dinner for the grown-ups and the older children. Many Romans go to bed as soon as it gets dark. They cannot afford to keep their oil lamps burning all evening.

Before Julius goes to sleep, he asks Titus to tell him a story — one of his favourites about the Trojan Wars. Titus tells it from memory. Books are expensive, as they have to be written by hand.

Now it is getting dark and the streets are becoming noisy. Julius can hear the horses and carts bringing goods to market. Suddenly he hears shouting and rushes to the window. A block of flats has caught fire. Firemen are rushing down the street with buckets of water and hoses. There are a lot of fires in Rome. Many flats are built of cheap materials, which catch fire easily. Oil lamps and open stoves can be dangerous.

Going shopping

In Julius's family, the slaves do most of the shopping. But today Julius is going shopping with his mother. He wants to buy a wedding present for his sister, Julia. She is getting married next month.

Julius's mother is buying some material for Julia's wedding dress. It is white silk. This is expensive as it comes all the way from China.

At the glass shop, Julius can see the craftsmen working at the back of the shop. He chooses a coloured glass bowl for his sister.

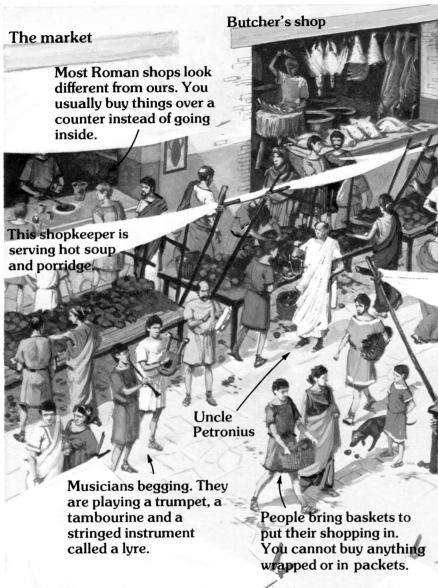

The market

Butcher's shop

Most Roman shops look different from ours. You usually buy things over a counter instead of going inside.

This shopkeeper is serving hot soup and porridge.

Uncle Petronius

Musicians begging. They are playing a trumpet, a tambourine and a stringed instrument called a lyre.

People bring baskets to put their shopping in. You cannot buy anything wrapped or in packets.

In Rome there are lots of different markets. Many of them are open every day. Some sell just fruit and vegetables. Others sell meat or fish. Julius sometimes goes to markets with his Uncle Petronius, who is a market inspector. His job is to check that the food is fresh and correctly weighed.

Stepping stones help you cross the street in wet weather.

This man has been arrested by a soldier for stealing fruit.

Advertisement

These men have no jobs. They queue up every day for free wheat. This is given by the government.

These men are painting an advertisement for the races, which will be held next week.

People pay for things with coins made of bronze, silver or gold. There is no paper money.

This stall is selling fruit called pomegranates. The Romans do not have potatoes or tomatoes. These come originally from South America and have not been discovered yet.

Next they go to the chemist's. Julius has hurt his knee. The chemist mixes an ointment of fat and herbs to put on it.

The togas are whitened over fires burning a chemical called sulphur.

The cloth is trodden in a special mixture to clean it.

A slave takes one of Antonius's togas to the cleaner's. Roman cleaners are called fullers. They use a kind of clay called fuller's earth to clean things.

Julia's wedding

Julia's nails are being painted.

Make-up

Perfume

Today is Julia's wedding day. Octavia and some of the slave women are helping her to get ready. She will wear a white dress and an orange veil with a crown of leaves. Julia is marrying a young nobleman called Lucius Philippus. Like all Roman marriages, it was arranged by the parents.

There is a short ceremony in front of the family shrine. Then the marriage contract is read and signed.

The door is decorated with garlands of leaves.

Lucius and his parents are waiting to greet Julia at the door.

The guests all join in a procession to the bride's new home. Two children take Julia by the hand. Two other children walk behind carrying her things. There are singers and musicians too. Julius leads the procession.

He holds a torch made of burning wood. This is meant to chase away evil spirits. Julia is going to live with Lucius's family. After a special ceremony at the doorway, she is carried into the house.

A big party is held in Lucius's house. The children are invited too, as it is a special occasion. Singers, dancers and other entertainers have been hired. Julius likes the acrobats best. The guests lie on couches and eat with their fingers. Slaves bring in huge dishes of food. There are lots of different courses. The slaves wipe the guests' fingers between courses. At the end of the party, everyone is given a special cake to take home with them. It is made of pastry, cooked in wine and wrapped in leaves.

Musicians

Acrobats

There are all kinds of different meat dishes, including wild boar, goat, venison (deer), ostriches and even stuffed mice.

Lobster

This slave is mixing wine and water in a jar called a krater. Everyone drinks this – even the children.

Stuffed pig's head

Uncle Claudius has just come back from fighting in Mesopotamia*. He has bought presents for everyone, including a board game for Julius.

*This is in the Middle East. 17

A public holiday

Today is a holiday, so Julius is not going to school. The Romans do not have weekends, but they have a lot of public holidays instead. This one is Saturnalia, the festival of the god Saturn. It takes place at about the same time as our Christmas and lasts for several days. Julius has been looking forward to it for a long time.

People decorate their houses, inside and out, with garlands of leaves.

The family give each other presents. Julius gets a hoop from his mother. Octavia is given a wooden doll. The slaves are given the day off and some pocket money to spend.

Their friends and neighbours join in a big procession. It goes to the temple of Saturn. A bull is killed on an altar. This is done as a present for the god.

In the evening there is a big party. Everyone joins in – even the slaves. Julius and his family serve them at supper. Roast baby pig is always eaten on this holiday.

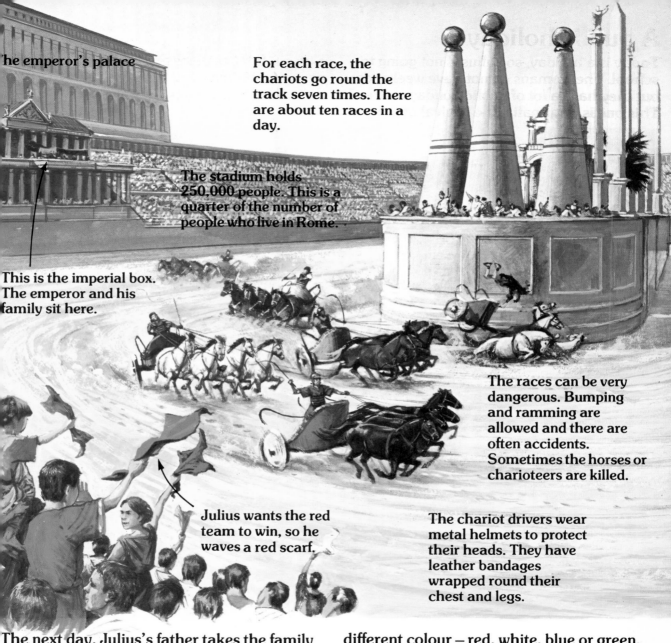

the emperor's palace

For each race, the chariots go round the track seven times. There are about ten races in a day.

The stadium holds 250,000 people. This is a quarter of the number of people who live in Rome.

This is the imperial box. The emperor and his family sit here.

The races can be very dangerous. Bumping and ramming are allowed and there are often accidents. Sometimes the horses or charioteers are killed.

Julius wants the red team to win, so he waves a red scarf.

The chariot drivers wear metal helmets to protect their heads. They have leather bandages wrapped round their chest and legs.

The next day, Julius's father takes the family to the races. They are held in a huge stadium called the Circus Maximus. Four teams of chariots take part. Each team wears a different colour – red, white, blue or green. There is a prize of money for the winner. It costs nothing to get in. Everyone tries to arrive early, in order to get the best seats.

19

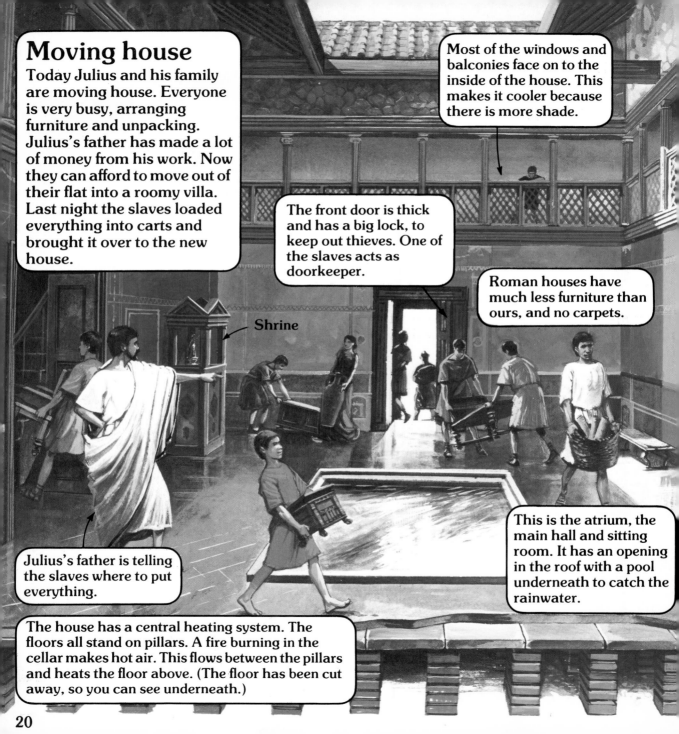

Moving house

Today Julius and his family are moving house. Everyone is very busy, arranging furniture and unpacking. Julius's father has made a lot of money from his work. Now they can afford to move out of their flat into a roomy villa. Last night the slaves loaded everything into carts and brought it over to the new house.

Most of the windows and balconies face on to the inside of the house. This makes it cooler because there is more shade.

The front door is thick and has a big lock, to keep out thieves. One of the slaves acts as doorkeeper.

Roman houses have much less furniture than ours, and no carpets.

Shrine

Julius's father is telling the slaves where to put everything.

This is the atrium, the main hall and sitting room. It has an opening in the roof with a pool underneath to catch the rainwater.

The house has a central heating system. The floors all stand on pillars. A fire burning in the cellar makes hot air. This flows between the pillars and heats the floor above. (The floor has been cut away, so you can see underneath.)

The house is still being decorated. An artist is painting a picture on one of the walls. He wets the plaster first and then paints on to it. He has an assistant to mix the paints.

The floor of the dining room is being covered with mosaics. These are designs made from tiny pieces of coloured stone. Julius is helping the artist to find the right colours.

The roof tiles are made of baked clay.

One of the things Julius likes best about the new house is the garden. There are trees and grapevines and a pool with a fountain. Julius's father has bought two new slaves to work as gardeners. They belonged to the last owner of the house.

Going on holiday

It is August now and very hot in Rome. Julius is going to stay with his grandparents in the country. His father is staying behind. He wants to supervise the decorators in the new house.

Octavia and her mother are travelling in a litter. It is carried by eight slaves.

Julius and his brother are riding on horseback. The luggage comes behind them in a cart.

The woods are full of animals, such as wild boar. These hunters are armed with spears. Guns have not been invented yet.

This coach is taking passengers to the cit

Slaves pull barges full of wheat up the river to Rome.

A few rich people hav their own carriages.

You can see tombstones along the road. No-one is buried inside the city.

This chariot is carrying the emperor's mail. There is no postal service for ordinary people.

Most Roman roads are straight. They only bend to go round a big hill.

These workmen are building a new road. They have a special instrument to show when the ground is level.

A farmer is taking vegetables to market in his cart.

The Roman mile is 1,000 paces long. (This is shorter than ours.) Each mile is marked by a milestone, like this one.

Most people travel on foot. They cannot afford any kind of transport.

In the afternoon they stop at Ostia, a seaside port. Julius watches the sailors load the ships with cargo. Some of the ships travel to far-away places, such as India.

Julius's grandparents live on a farm. It is about two days' journey away. The family spend the night at an inn on the way.

Staying in the country

The farm is about five miles from the nearest village. To get there, they have to travel down a long, dusty road. It is a busy time on the farm. The wheat is nearly ready for harvesting. As they arrive, they see slaves picking grapes and olives. Most of the grapes will be made into wine. The olives will be used to make oil. About 100 slaves work on the farm. There are cattle, sheep, geese and chickens too. Julius's father will join them in a few weeks. They will stay until the end of September.

Beehives for making honey.

The slaves sleep here.

These men are collecting olives in baskets.

Stables

Oil and wine are stored in jars dug into the ground.

Julius's cousins have come to stay too. One of them is learning to swim. He uses a float made of reeds to hold on to.

Grandfather spends a lot of time fishing.

The cart will take the olives back to the farm to be crushed.

Picking grapes

Index